UKULELE
Chord Melody Solos

by Eric Cutshall

PLAYBACK+
Speed • Pitch • Balance • Loop

To access audio visit:
www.halleonard.com/mylibrary

Enter Code
3632-5428-0791-2239

ISBN 978-1-4584-1853-1

HAL•LEONARD®
7777 W. BLUEMOUND RD. P.O. BOX 13819 MILWAUKEE, WI 53213

Visit Hal Leonard Online at
www.halleonard.com

Introduction

This book is designed to introduce you to the chord melody style of playing the ukulele. The term "chord melody" refers to the act of playing chords and melody simultaneously on one instrument. This book is full of tips and instructions on how to create your own chord melody arrangements. Several popular songs are covered, and most have detailed explanations on how the arrangement was created. This book can also be used strictly as a songbook, in which case you would just play the songs and ignore the notes (no pun intended).

Some experience with the ukulele will be helpful, as the arrangements contain a mixture of solo notes and chords. However, even if you're a total beginner, this book can still provide education and enjoyment. The arrangements range in difficulty from elementary to advanced, so there's really something for everyone.

The songs are written in both tablature and standard music notation. Knowing how to read music is important if you plan on creating your own arrangements in a chord melody style. Sheet music and songbooks are excellent sources of material in this regard, but most are written in standard notation. If you don't know how to read music, I suggest you purchase the *Hal Leonard Ukulele Method: Book 1*. Not only does it teach music reading, but it also covers melody playing, basic chords, strumming, reading tablature, and much more. The book also introduces you to its author, Lil' Rev, who's a fantastic ukulele player. To help get you started, I've included a note chart at the end of the book that shows the name of each note on the tab staff and its corresponding note on the notation staff.

About the Author

Eric Cutshall grew up in a musical family. At an early age, he began to play with a few of the instruments lying around the house, including the guitar, ukulele, and banjo. His interests later expanded to mandolin, Dobro, lap steel, and dulcimer, and he received private music lessons throughout junior high and high school. After graduating, he continued his musical education at Musicians Institute in Hollywood, California.

Eric has been a professional musician and music teacher for over twenty years. In addition to live performances throughout the United States and Europe, he's been featured on several recordings, including *Cost of Living* by the Broke String Band, *Over the Edge* and *Last Wave of the Day* by the Reckless Reefers, and his solo CD *Banjo on My Knee*. He wrote *Mandolin Christmas* (Centerstream Publications, distributed by Hal Leonard). All CDs or individual songs are available at cdbaby.com. For more information about future books or CDs, please visit his website: www.eric-cutshall.com.

Eric currently lives with his wife and their dog in a cozy cabin located in the beautiful San Bernardino Mountains of Southern California.

Essential Terms & Concepts

Before we get into the arrangements, let's look at a few essential terms or concepts you'll need to be familiar with in order to get the most out of this book.

Chord Variations

In order to successfully play chord melody style on the ukulele, you need to be able to harmonize notes in many ways. To *harmonize* a note simply means to play a chord beneath it. The chord we use to harmonize a note usually includes that note within it, which is the main reason it sounds good. When we harmonize notes on the ukulele, the melody note usually appears on the first or second string. This means we need to be able to play a variety of chords so that we can find one with the appropriate note on top.

This is where the subject of *chord variations* comes in. Look at the first row of chords below. They're all F chords in first position, but they each contain a different note on top. In the first chord, an A note is on top. In the second chord, we simply mute the first string so it doesn't sound at all, leaving the F on string 2 as the highest note. (**Note:** Due to the tuning of the ukulele, this isn't technically true. The A note on string 4 is actually higher in pitch than the F note on string 2, but for our purposes, we'll be placing the melodies notes on strings 1 and 2, so we'll think of those notes as the "highest.") In the third chord, we add the third fret on string 1, making C the highest note in the chord.

By doing this, we have three different versions of an F chord, each with a different note on top: F, A, or C. Consequently, these are the three different notes that make up an F chord (triad). F is called the root, A is the 3rd, and C is the 5th. If we were only accompanying ourselves with the ukulele while singing, then the standard F chord would do just fine all the time. But if we want to play the melody as well as the chords, then we need to be able to rearrange chord tones like this.

But what if the melody note is not contained in the normal chord? Well, we have a few different options. We can play the note by itself as a *single note*. We can find another note that sounds good with it, which is called a *harmony note*. Or we can reharmonize the note altogether with a totally different chord that contains the melody note. This is known as a *chord substitution*. You'll find examples of all three options in the arrangements here, with chord substitutions playing more of a role in the intermediate and advanced arrangements.

In the second row, we see a few other chord variations on first-position chords. In this instance, though, the second voicing of each chord is technically incomplete, as it does not contain all three different notes (or in the case of D7, all four different notes) that normally make up the chord. The second C chord, for example, only contains one C note (the root) and two G notes (the 5th). This is sometimes referred to as C5, which indicates that the 3rd is not present. The 3rd is not present in the final G chord either, making it a G5. In the second D7 chord, we have the notes A, C, F#, and A. We're missing the D note, which makes this a "rootless" voicing. Though we generally try to harmonize the melody notes with complete chords, this is not always possible, and in those cases, we may resort to these incomplete versions. Alternatively, we may simply choose these voicings for a different sound.

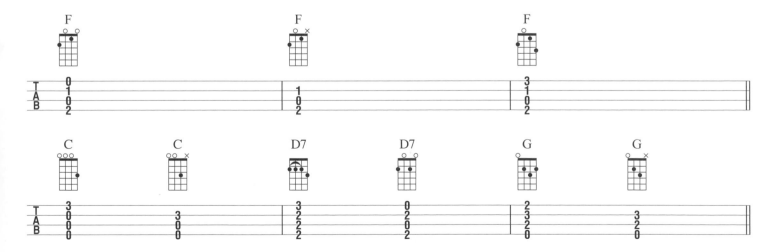

Lead Sheet

A *lead sheet* is a piece of music that includes the melody and chords to a song. Often the lyrics are included as well. They're very handy when you need to "fake" an accompaniment to a song that you don't know very well or may have even never heard. However, they're also useful when creating chord melody versions of a song, which is our intent here. The first step to playing chord melody style is to learn the melody. Once you have it down, play through the accompanying chords. Make sure you're comfortable with those two elements before attempting to arrange your own version of a song in a chord melody style.

The first arrangement in this book, seen in the following chapter, is "Eight Days a Week," which is a well known song by The Beatles that you've probably heard a time or two. (In case you didn't know, George Harrison was also a ukulele player.) Before we get to the arrangement, though, let's first take a look at a sample lead sheet for the song. The song's originally in the key of D, but we've transposed it here to the key of F to make it easily playable on the uke. Transposing songs is extremely common due to different vocal ranges, and lead sheets make this process quick. Although most lead sheets feature the melody written in standard notation only, I've included tablature in this one for your convenience.

TRACK 1

Eight Days a Week

Words and Music by John Lennon and Paul McCartney

Easy Arrangements

Eight Days a Week

Now let's take a look at our first chord melody arrangement. I kept this version basic to show you how to get started with your own arrangements. I used a combination of chords and single notes throughout.

Verse (8 measures):

- The first chord is an F with an A melody note, so I use a first-position F chord, which has the A note on the open first string.

- I start measure 2 with an incomplete first-position G chord, because the melody note is actually on the second string.

- The melody in measure 3 ascends up through the notes of the B♭ chord. I begin with the melody note only on string 3 and then continue stacking notes on top as the melody rises.

- Measure 4 contains only one A note, so the open first-position F chord from measure 1 works well. These four measures repeat to complete the verse.

Chorus (8 measures):

- Measure 9 starts with an open Dm chord, which contains the melody note (A) on the first string.

- Measure 10 starts with a B♭6 chord. The melody note, G, is located on the third fret of the second string. This is the sixth note in a B♭ scale. If you add a G note to a B♭ chord, you have a B♭6 chord. This is the type of music theory knowledge that's very helpful when arranging chord melody style solos.

- Measure 11 is the same as measure 9.

- Measure 12 starts with a first-position G chord. The first string is omitted, though, because the melody note is G, which is on the second string.

- Measure 13 starts with a first-position F chord with the melody note, A, on the first string.

- Measure 14 is the same as measure 12.

- A first-position B♭ chord is played three times in measure 15, with the B♭ melody note on string 1.

- Measure 16 starts with a first-position F chord with the A melody note on the first string. An incomplete first-position F chord completes the measure, in which the first and fourth strings are omitted, since the melody note, F, is now on the second string.

Bridge (8 measures):

- The bridge begins in measure 17 with a C chord, which has been simplified to a C5 chord to support the G melody note on string 2.

- Measure 18 contains the same chord.

- Measure 19 is all single notes, which take place over a Dm harmony that we've chosen to omit.

- Measure 20 contains an incomplete, two-string Dm chord with the first melody note, G, on the second string. Note that G is not a chord tone of Dm, but it's quickly resolved to F, which is the 3rd of Dm.

- Measures 21 and 22 both contain incomplete first-position G chords (G5 really) with the melody notes on string 2 and 1.

- Measure 23 is all single notes, which take place over a B♭ harmony that we've chosen to omit (as we did in measure 19).

- Measure 24 begins with an incomplete C chord and finishes with a first-position C7 chord.

Eight Days a Week

Words and Music by John Lennon and Paul McCartney

TRACK 2

Bridge

Eight days a week, I love _____ you.

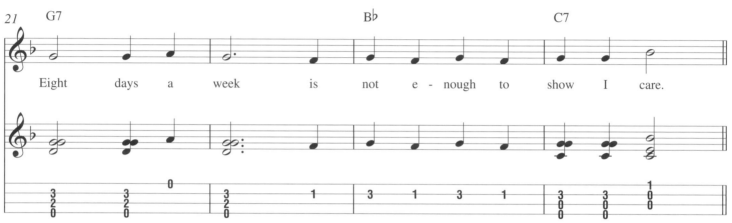

Eight days a week is not e-nough to show I care.

Verse

2. Love you ev-ry day girl, al-ways on my mind.

D.S. al Fine

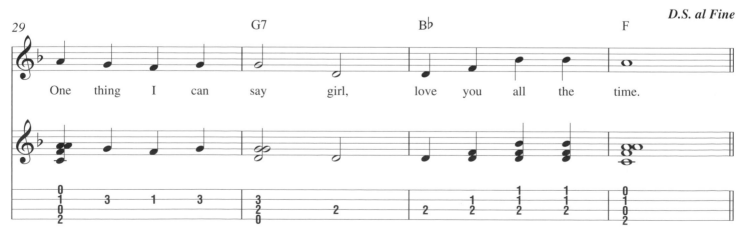

One thing I can say girl, love you all the time.

Tiny Bubbles

This arrangement contains first-position chords and single notes as well as *intervals*, which are two notes played together. This is the same as harmonizing a melody note with one other note. We'll see a good deal of chord variations as well. The use of intervals and chord variations is a great alternative to using so many single notes. I'll explain the measures that have variations.

Verse (16 measures):

- The song starts with pickup notes using a first-position F chord. Measure one starts with the same F chord, but this time it's incomplete, because the melody note starts on the second string. On beat 2, we play strings 3 and 4 of the F chord. These are called intervals or partial chords. In the case of the latter, the melody is on string 3, and a harmony note (interval) is on string 4.

- Measures 3 and 4 contain a simplified C5 substitute for C, which was also featured in "Eight Days a Week." Even though three strings are strummed, only two different notes are sounded, as strings 4 and 2 contain G notes played an octave apart.

- Measure 5 contains a thinned-out variation of a C chord, and measure 6 has C6 and C5 chords. C6 is the easiest chord to play on the ukulele as it contains all four open strings. Remember that all these C chord variations are substituting for the overall C7 harmony in order to accommodate the different melody notes.

- Measure 10 has an F chord with the fourth string omitted.

- Measure 11 has a first-position B♭ chord played with all four strings followed by a single melody note.

- Measure 12 has a first-position B♭ minor chord followed by single melody notes F and G on string 2.

- Measure 13 has a first-position F chord followed by a variation of the same chord. For the second F chord, we've added a C note on the third fret of string 1 to accommodate the C melody note.

- Measure 14 starts with a two-string version of a C chord (strings 3 and 2) followed by a C6 chord that we get from adding the open first string to the chord we already had.

Bridge (8 measures):

- Measure 17 starts with two notes of a B♭ chord and then adds a third note.

- Measure 19 follows this same process with an F chord.

- Various G7 forms and incomplete G chords appear in measure 21 and 22.

Tiny Bubbles

Words and Music by Leon Pober

TRACK 3

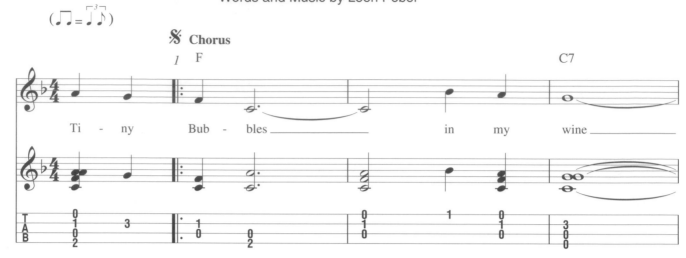

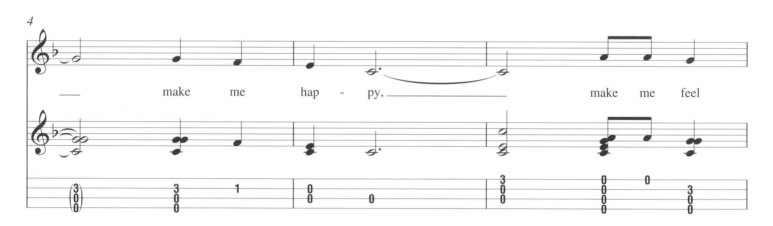

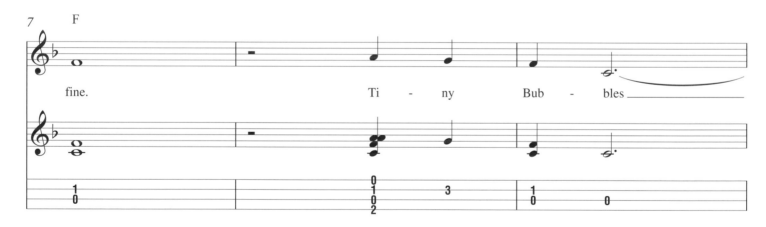

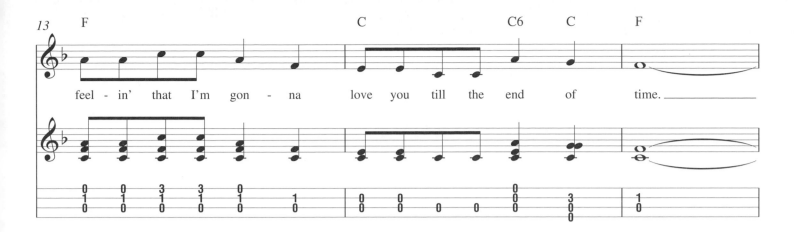

feel - in' that I'm gon - na love you till the end of time. ____

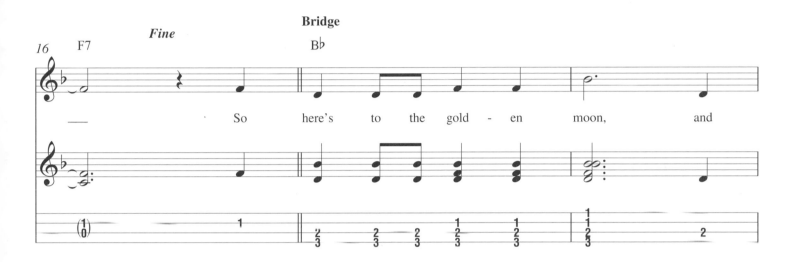

So here's to the gold - en moon, and

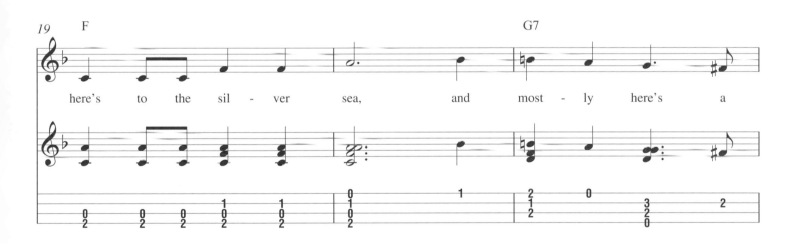

here's to the sil - ver sea, and most - ly here's a

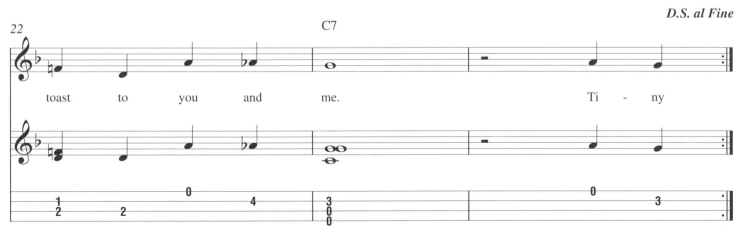

toast to you and me. Ti - ny

Aloha Oe

This is another simple arrangement that's similar to "Tiny Bubbles." We're mixing single notes, chord variations, and intervals.

Chord Inversions

The arrangements in this chapter feature *chord inversions*. Chords consist of three (or more) notes. A three-note chord is called a *triad*. Each triad can be played in three different positions on the ukulele. Let's take a look at how this works with a D chord. For simplicity's sake, we'll play notes on strings 3, 2, and 1 only since there are only three different notes in a triad. This way, we won't be doubling any notes; we'll play only the three different notes of the triad.

Root Position

The notes in a D chord are D (the root), F# (the major 3rd), and A (the 5th). If we play our open D chord, we say that this chord is in *root position*, because the root (D) is on the bottom.

First Inversion

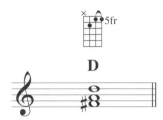

Now if we take that bottom note, D, and move it up an octave, we'll need to move up the neck to find a position for the other two notes (F# and A). We end up with this voicing in fifth position. This form has the 3rd (F#) in the bottom and is called *first inversion*.

Second Inversion

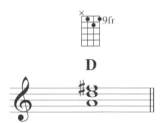

Repeating that process one more time leaves us with this voicing, which is called *second inversion*. It has the 5th (A) in the bottom.

By doing this, we're simply playing the same notes rearranged in a different order. This allows us to accommodate different melody notes on the first or second strings in various positions on the neck, which is extremely helpful when arranging songs in the chord melody style.

This may seem a little daunting at first. But remember that any of these voicings can be moved up or down the neck to play chords of another root. For example, our second inversion D chord from above can be moved down two frets to play a second inversion C chord. The shape of the chord is the same, but the name (and sound) changes.

There are several songs in this book that make use of these inversions. Learning these songs will help you become familiar with the concept. Also remember to consult the note chart in the back of the book if you're having trouble finding a particular note or chord.

There are, of course, more chords and other ways to play the ones in this book. I suggest purchasing the *Hal Leonard Ukulele Chord Finder*. Not only does it display three voicings for every chord you'll ever need, but it also contains several pages explaining chord construction. That book will serve you well in arranging your own chord melody versions of songs. Further studies in books on music theory and chord construction will make arranging easier and also open new doors to more exciting and complex arrangements. Private lessons with a professional music instructor that's well versed in music theory would also be very helpful. The internet is a great resource for meeting fellow ukulele players who might be able to suggest a good instructor. And even though this book is geared toward solo ukulele, playing or "jamming" with other musicians is also a great way to improve your skills and learn more songs. There seem to be a lot of ukulele clubs forming these days. If there's not one in your area yet, you could always start one! I've learned many things over the years by interacting with other musicians.

All I Have to Do Is Dream

This arrangement of the classic Everly Brothers song features inversions of Dm, C, B♭, Am, and G7 chords. The fourth string was left out of some chords so that it would not interfere with the melody.

TRACK 5

All I Have to Do Is Dream
Words and Music by Boudleaux Bryant

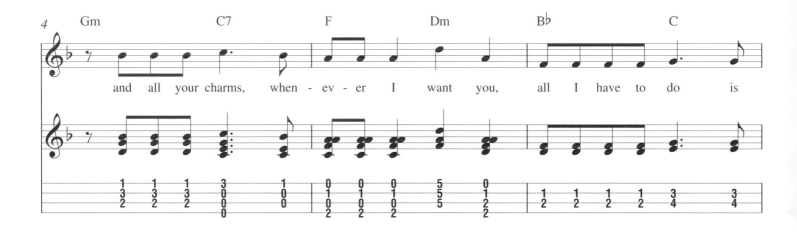

Additional lyrics

2. When I feel blue in the night,
   When I need you to hold me tight,
   Whenever I want you, all I have to do is dream.

Surfer Girl

The chord inversions in this Beach Boys classic include B♭, C7, and F6. A Cadd9 chord is also featured in the bridge. This is a C chord with an added D note. I chose a B♭m6 chord in measures 4 and 22 instead of a B♭ minor chord because I liked the way it sounded. Ultimately, your ear and personal taste will be the final judge of which chords you use in your own arrangements.

Surfer Girl
Written by Brian Wilson
TRACK 6

Tennessee Waltz

This country western classic was also a hit on the pop charts. Look for inversions of C, E7, and F6 chords.

Tennessee Waltz

Words and Music by Redd Stewart and Pee Wee King

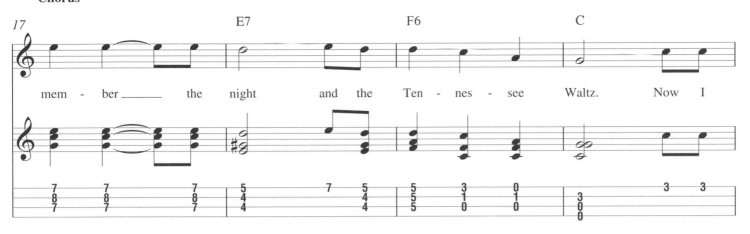

mem - ber _____ the night and the Ten - nes - see Waltz. Now I

know just _____ how much I have lost. _____ Yes 2. I

Verse

lost my lit - tle dar - ling the ____ night they were ___ play - ing _____ the

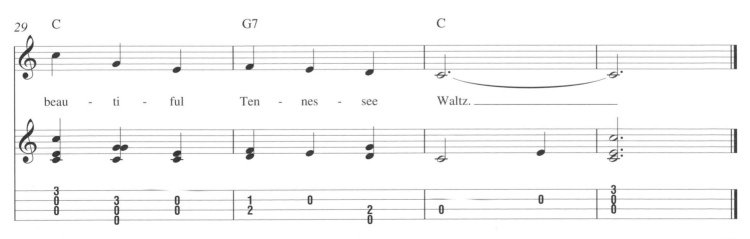

beau - ti - ful Ten - nes - see Waltz. _____

Love Me Tender

If the melody of "Love Me Tender" sounds familiar, it's because it was originally a song called "Aura Lee." In this arrangement, I used inversions of D, Fmaj7, Fm, Fm6, C, and E chords.

TRACK 8

Love Me Tender
Words and Music by Elvis Presley and Vera Matson

Additional lyrics

2. Love me tender, love me long;
   Take me to your heart.
   For it's there that I belong,
   And we'll never part.

Chorus: Love me tender, love me dear;
   Tell me you are mine.
   I'll be yours through all the years
   Till the end of time.

Combining Chord Positions

Sometimes you can combine different chord positions to get a different sound or to make certain chord transitions easier. The four arrangements in this chapter demonstrate this concept.

Nights in White Satin

Notice the G chord in measure 3. We briefly add an D note on top at fret 5 in place of the B at fret 2 to accommodate the melody. We're not shifting chord positions, but we're reaching up to a melody note that would normally be part of a different chord position, briefly creating a G5 voicing. I also make use of another add9 chord, Dadd9, in measure 11. This is the same chord form we used for Cadd9 in "Surfer Girl."

TRACK 9

Nights in White Satin
Words and Music by Justin Hayward

Additional lyrics

2. Gazing at people, some hand in hand,
   Just what I'm going through they can't understand.
   Some try to tell me, thoughts they cannot defend.
   Just what you want to be, you will be in the end.
   And love you, yes I love you,
   Oh how I love you, oh how I love you.

Stand by Me

In this 1961 #1 hit for Ben E. King, I once again used the G5 chord from "Nights in White Satin." I also make use of a seventh-position G chord (measure 16) that's built from the open C chord form.

TRACK 10

Stand by Me

Words and Music by Jerry Leiber, Mike Stoller and Ben E. King

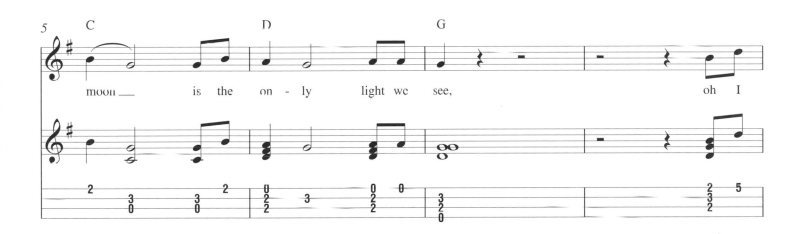

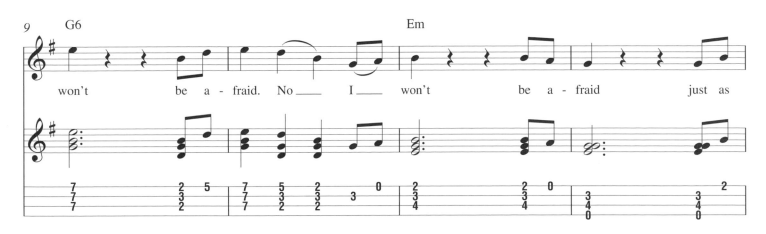

Additional lyrics

2. If the sky that we look upon should tumble and fall,
   Or the mountains should crumble to the sea.
   I won't cry, I won't cry. No I won't shed a tear,
   Just as long as you stand, stand by me.

Unchained Melody

The combination G5 chord also appears in this popular ballad from the Righteous Brothers. I also used the seventh-position G chord (and a G7 variant) from "Stand by Me."

Unchained Melody

TRACK 11

Lyric by Hy Zaret
Music by Alex North

need your love,   I   need your love.   God

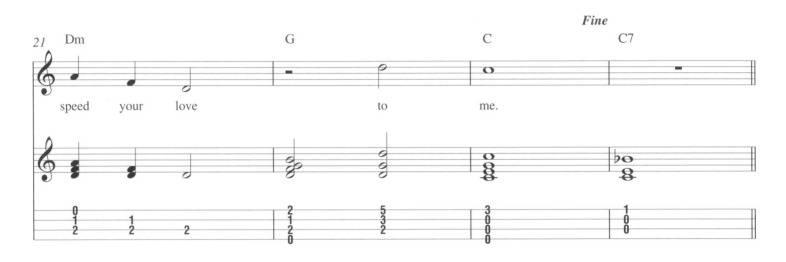

Fine

speed   your   love   to   me.

Bridge

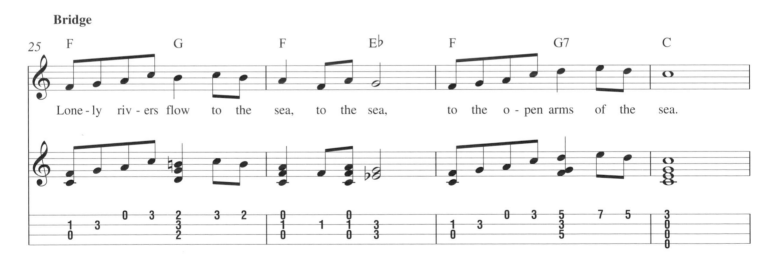

Lone - ly riv - ers flow to the sea, to the sea, to the o - pen arms of the sea.

D.C. al Fine

Lone - ly riv - ers sigh, "Wait for me, wait for me!" I'll be com - ing home; wait for me.

Ring of Fire

This song was the biggest hit of Johnny Cash's career, staying at #1 on the charts for seven weeks in 1963. The G5 chord is featured again in the chorus. The original song actually features several time signature changes, but in this arrangement there's only one measure of 2/4. Be sure to watch out for it!

TRACK 12

Ring of Fire

Words and Music by Merle Kilgore and June Carter

Additional lyrics

2. The taste of love is sweet
When hearts like ours meet
I fell for you like a child
Oh, but the fire went wild

Enhancing Basic Arrangements

In this chapter, we're going to look at how we take a basic arrangement of Beethoven's "Ode to Joy" and enhance it with various techniques. The first arrangement is quite basic and uses single notes and first-position chords. The second version is more challenging and contains more chords and fewer single notes. Among the additional chords are a second-position D chord in measures 2, 6, and 14 as well as the combination G5 voicing from previous songs in measures 1, 5, and 13. Again, knowledge of chord construction allowed me to replace single notes with added chords in the enhanced version. I know I've already mentioned this book, but the *Hal Leonard Ukulele Chord Finder* contains a wonderful explanation of chord construction as well as three different versions of each chord—extremely valuable information with regards to chord melody style.

Learn the basic arrangement first and then try the second version. Remember that, when arranging a chord melody version of a song, it's always best to learn the melody first and then the chords. I tend to use a mixture of chords and single notes as well as harmony notes to get a variety of sounds.

The enhanced version of "Ode to Joy" may be difficult at first, as there are a few quick chord changes and new chords. If you encounter any particularly difficult areas, practice them several times slowly and accurately. Once you have them securely under your fingers at a slow tempo, begin to increase the speed until you're able to play them at tempo. Also, try to memorize the names of any new chord shapes that you learn!

Ode to Joy – Basic Arrangement

TRACK 13

Ode to Joy

By Ludwig van Beethoven

Ode to Joy – Enhanced Arrangement

Ode to Joy

By Ludwig van Beethoven

Ascending and Descending Chord Patterns

In this chapter, we'll take a look at a couple of tricks you can employ when you have a static chord that lasts for more than one measure: *ascending* or *descending chord patterns*. These can add a great deal of sophistication to your arrangements that will help them from sounding ordinary.

I Can't Help It (If I'm Still in Love with You)

We'll use an arrangement of the country standard "I Can't Help It (If I'm Still in Love with You)" to demonstrate how the ascending chord pattern works. The verse is fairly straightforward with a mixture of mostly chords and a few single notes. There are a few higher-position chords included, such as the $B\flat$ in measure 3 and the F6 in measure 4, but other than that, there's not much new here.

In the bridge, however, things begin to get interesting. Take a look at measures 12 and 13; the melody note (D) never changes. And though a $B\flat$ chord would work for these two measures, I used an ascending chord pattern to provide some movement and avoid a bit of monotony. Basically, I change one note at a time in the chord, and this changes the name and sound while keeping the melody note the same. Let's examine it more closely.

The melody note is D, and the accompaniment chord is normally $B\flat$. For beats 1 and 2 of measure 12, I stayed with the usual $B\flat$ chord. I put the melody note (D) on the first string at the fifth fret and added the $B\flat$ on string 4, fret 3 and the F on string 2, fret 1. The third string is not played at all. For beats 3 and 4, I simply raised the F note a half step to F$\sharp$ by moving from the first fret on string 2 to the second fret. This raised the 5th of the chord, which changes the $B\flat$ chord into a $B\flat$+, or $B\flat$ augmented: $B\flat$–D–F$\sharp$. (An augmented triad is a major triad with a raised 5th.) For beats 1 and 2 of measure 13, I moved the F$\sharp$ note up another half step to G at the third fret. This creates a $B\flat$6 chord: $B\flat$–D–G. For beat 3, I moved the G at the third fret up to A$\flat$ on the fourth fret, which creates a $B\flat$7 chord: $B\flat$–D–(F)–A$\flat$. Note that, even though the 5th (F) is not present in this chord, it's still a $B\flat$7 chord, as the 5th is optional.

To play these chord shapes, pluck strings 4, 2, and 1 simultaneously instead of strumming through all the strings. You want to avoid the third string sounding out. Use your thumb for the fourth string, your index finger for string 2, and your middle finger for string 1. For the last chord in measure 13, I chose a B diminished seventh chord, which is represented by the °7 in the music. Again, this did not change the D melody note, but it creates a nice transition into the following F6 chord. Notice that this entire pattern appears again in measures 20-21. I would not have been able to arrange these two measures like this without some knowledge in music theory.

I Can't Help It (If I'm Still in Love with You)

Words and Music by Hank Williams

Additional lyrics

2. Somebody else stood by your side,
   And he looked so satisfied.
   And I can't help it if I'm still in love with you.

Bridge
It's hard to know another's lips will kiss you
And hold you just the way I used to do.
Heaven only knows how much I miss you.
I can't help it if I'm still in love with you.

Blue Skies

To demonstrate descending chord patterns, let's check out an arrangement of "Blue Skies." It actually begins right off the bat with a descending chord pattern in the intro.

I start with a three-string version of an E minor chord, which contains E, G, and B notes, low to high. For the next chord, I lower the E note a half step, or one fret, to D♯, while the other two notes remain the same. This is a good time to bring up the fact that there are some chords that have more than one correct name; this new chord is one of them. I've labeled it B+/D♯, which is read "B augmented over D♯." This is shorthand for a B+ chord with D♯ (the 3rd) as the lowest note. If you really paid attention in the chapter on inversions, you'll be able to lable this as a first-inversion B+ chord.

For the next chord, I lowered the note on the third string (D♯) again by a half step to the second fret. The chord now created is an inverted G chord, with the 5th in the bottom. This would make it a second-inversion G chord. I continue the process one more time by lowering the D to C♯ on the first fret. This creates another chord with more than one name. I call it a C♯m7♭5, which means C♯ minor 7 with a flatted fifth. (This is one of my favorite chords.) This two-measure phrase repeats to complete the four-measure intro.

The chords in the verse are the same as in the intro, but the *harmonic rhythm*—i.e., the speed at which the chords change—has slowed down, so that each chord lasts a full measure instead of only two beats. Throughout the arrangement, I mix chords and single notes for variety. I also use octaves in measures 9–10 and 17–18 to provide more interest. The melody note falls on the third string, and the octave played on the first string produces a fuller sound. Remember this trick in your own arrangements. There where also times when the melody note landed on the first string and I omitted the fourth string because I felt the chord sounded better. You'll make your own judgments in this regard when you create your own arrangements.

Blue Skies

Words and Music by Irving Berlin

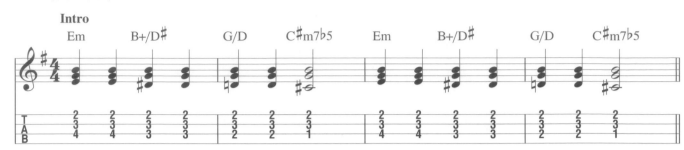

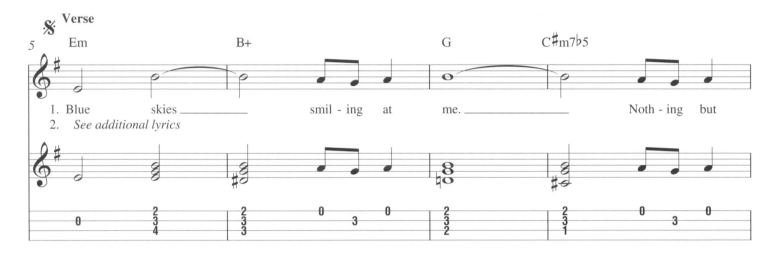

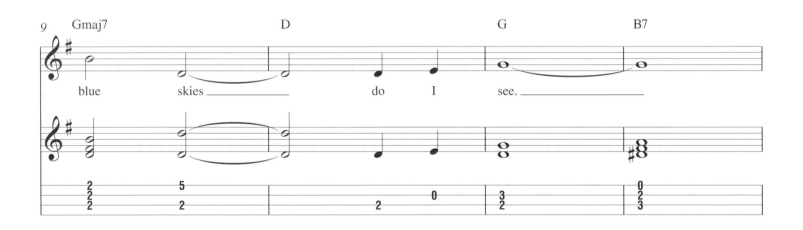

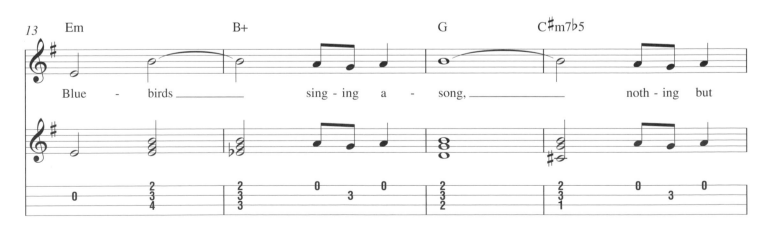

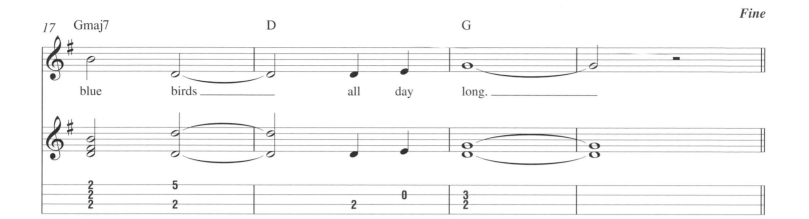

blue birds _____ all day long. _____

Bridge

Nev - er saw the sun shin - ing so bright, nev - er saw things go - ing so right.

No - tic - ing the days hur - ry - ing by; when you're in love, my how they fly.

Additional lyrics

2. Blue days, all of them gone.
   Nothing but blue skies from now on.
   Blue skies smiling at me.
   Nothing but blue skies do I see.

Advanced Arrangements

To finish up our chord melody journey, we'll look at two advanced arrangements. They introduce some chords that may not be quite as familiar to you, and they include more chord positions and inversions than our earlier arrangements. Both of the songs are considered jazz standards.

Georgia on My Mind

Hoagy Carmichael wrote this song in 1930, and Ray Charles immortalized it with his famous 1960 recording. Measure 8 features a C+ (C augmented), which resolves nicely to an F chord. Measure 11 features two of my favorite chords used in a wonderful combination: Em7♭5 (E minor seven flat five) followed by A+. These two chords make a nice transition into the bridge, which starts with a D minor chord. Some measures of this arrangement contain a chord change every beat. If there are any chords you are unfamiliar with, be sure to spend some extra time practicing them.

Georgia on My Mind

TRACK 17

Words by Stuart Gorrell
Music by Hoagy Carmichael

Verse

1. Geor - gia __ Geor - gia, __ the whole day through. Just an
2. *See additional lyrics*

old sweet song keeps Geor - gia on my mind. (Geor - gia on my mind.)

moon - light through the pines. ___

Bridge

Oth - er arms __ reach out to me; __ oth - er eyes __ smile ten - der - ly __

Additional lyrics

2. Georgia, Georgia, a song of you
   Comes as sweet and clear as moonlight through the pines.

Satin Doll

"Satin Doll" was first recorded in 1953 by Duke Ellington, who co-wrote the song along with Billy Strayhorn and Johnny Mercer. It features some unusual chord changes and some others that are found quite often in jazz music. An Asus4 chord (suspended fourth) first appears in measure 5. Instead of containing the root, 3rd, and 5th like a normal major triad, this chord is constructed with the root, 4th, and 5th. I chose this chord because the melody note is D, which is the fourth note in an A major scale. Measures 7 and 8 consist of a *turnaround* (C–Dm–Em–A7), which leads us back to the beginning of the song on the Dm chord.

A Gsus4 is used in measures 11 and 12 to accommodate the C melody note on beat 1. The chords used in measures 13 and 14 (Fmaj7, F#°7, Gm, and C7) are often used as a turnaround or an intro to a song. In this case, I use the chords to spice up the arrangement while the melody holds out one note. I use a G+ chord in measure 18 to lead back to the beginning of the song.

Satin Doll

TRACK 18

By Duke Ellington

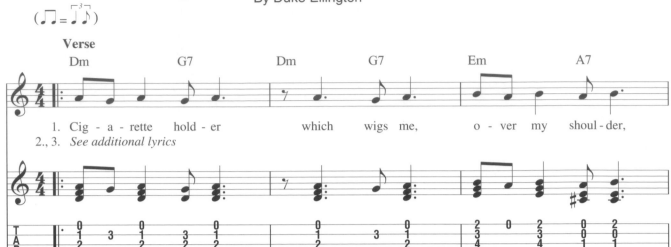

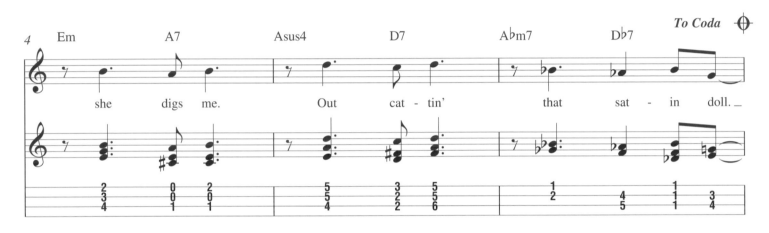

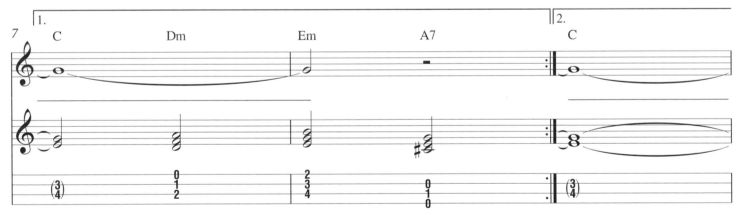

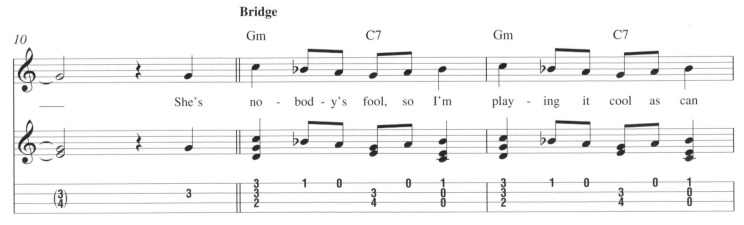

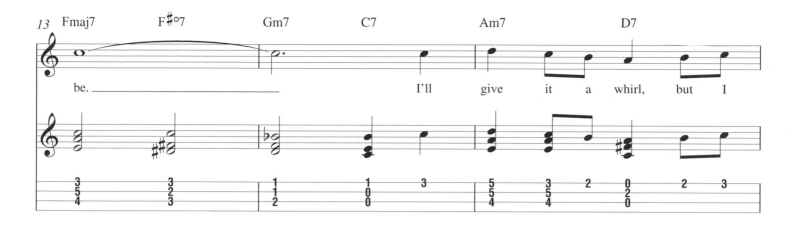

be. _____ I'll give it a whirl, but I

D.C. al Coda

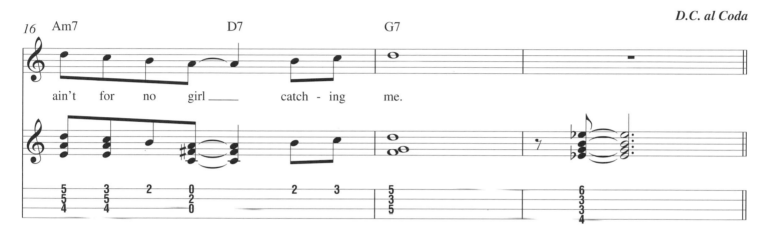

ain't for no girl _____ catch - ing me.

⊕ **Coda**

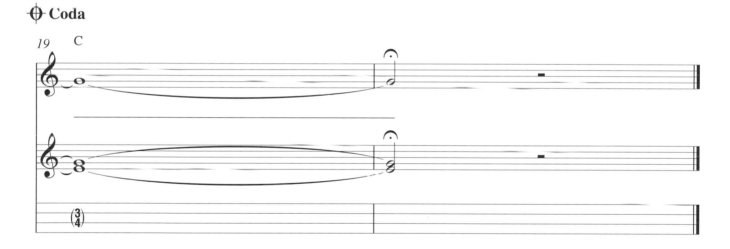

Additional lyrics

2. Baby shall we go out skippin'?
   Careful amigo; you're flippin'.
   Speaks Latin, that satin doll.

3. Telephone numbers, well you know.
   Doing my rhumbas with uno.
   And that'n my satin doll.

Note Chart

1st string

2nd string

3rd string

4th string

Here is a blank manuscript page. You can use it to make notes on some of the arrangements in this book, or you can start some of your own arrangements.

The Best Collections for Ukulele

The Best Songs Ever

70 songs have now been arranged for ukulele. Includes: Always • Bohemian Rhapsody • Memory • My Favorite Things • Over the Rainbow • Piano Man • What a Wonderful World • Yesterday • You Raise Me Up • and more.

00282413 . . . . $17.99

Campfire Songs for Ukulele

30 favorites to sing as you roast marshmallows and strum your uke around the campfire. Includes: God Bless the U.S.A. • Hallelujah • The House of the Rising Sun • I Walk the Line • Puff the Magic Dragon • Wagon Wheel • You Are My Sunshine • and more.

00129170 . . . . $14.99

The Daily Ukulele

arr. Liz and Jim Beloff
Strum a different song everyday with easy arrangements of 365 of your favorite songs in one big songbook! Includes favorites by the Beatles, Beach Boys, and Bob Dylan, folk songs, pop songs, kids' songs, Christmas carols, and Broadway and Hollywood tunes, all with a spiral binding for ease of use.

00240356 Original Edition $39.99
00240681 Leap Year Edition $39.99
00119270 Portable Edition $37.50

Disney Hits for Ukulele

Play 23 of your favorite Disney songs on your ukulele. Includes: The Bare Necessities • Cruella De Vil • Do You Want to Build a Snowman? • Kiss the Girl • Lava • Let It Go • Once upon a Dream • A Whole New World • and more.

00151250 . . . . $16.99

Also available:

00291547 **Disney Fun Songs for Ukulele** . . . $16.99
00701708 **Disney Songs for Ukulele** $14.99
00334696 **First 50 Disney Songs on Ukulele** . $16.99

First 50 Songs You Should Play on Ukulele

An amazing collec-tion of 50 accessible, must-know favorites: Edelweiss • Hey, Soul Sister • I Walk the Line • I'm Yours • Imagine • Over the Rainbow • Peaceful Easy Feeling • The Rainbow Connection • Riptide • more.

00149250 . . . . $16.99

Also available:

00292082 **First 50 Melodies on Ukulele** . . . $15.99
00289029 **First 50 Songs on Solo Ukulele** . . $15.99
00347437 **First 50 Songs to Strum on Uke** . $16.99

40 Most Streamed Songs for Ukulele

40 top hits that sound great on uke! Includes: Despacito • Feel It Still • Girls like You • Happier • Havana • High Hopes • The Middle • Perfect • 7 Rings • Shallow • Shape of You • Something Just like This • Stay • Sucker • Sunflower • Sweet but Psycho • Thank U, Next • There's Nothing Holdin' Me Back • Without Me • and more!

00298113 . . . . $17.99

The 4 Chord Songbook

With just 4 chords, you can play 50 hot songs on your ukulele! Songs include: Brown Eyed Girl • Do Wah Diddy Diddy • Hey Ya! • Ho Hey • Jessie's Girl • Let It Be • One Love • Stand by Me • Toes • With or Without You • and many more.

00142050 . . . . $16.99

Also available:

00141143 **The 3-Chord Songbook** $16.99

Pop Songs for Kids

30 easy pop favorites for kids to play on uke, including: Brave • Can't Stop the Feeling! • Feel It Still • Fight Song • Happy • Havana • House of Gold • How Far I'll Go • Let It Go • Remember Me (Ernesto de la Cruz) • Rewrite the Stars • Roar • Shake It Off • Story of My Life • What Makes You Beautiful • and more.

00284415 . . . . $16.99

Simple Songs for Ukulele

50 favorites for standard G-C-E-A ukulele tuning, including: All Along the Watchtower • Can't Help Falling in Love • Don't Worry, Be Happy • Ho Hey • I'm Yours • King of the Road • Sweet Home Alabama • You Are My Sunshine • and more.

00156815 . . . . $14.99

Also available:

00276644 **More Simple Songs for Ukulele** . $14.99

Top Hits of 2020

18 uke-friendly tunes of 2020 are featured in this collection of melody, lyric and chord arrangements in standard G-C-E-A tuning. Includes: Adore You (Harry Styles) • Before You Go (Lewis Capaldi) • Cardigan (Taylor Swift) • Daisies (Katy Perry) • I Dare You (Kelly Clarkson) • Level of Concern (twenty one pilots) • No Time to Die (Billie Eilish) • Rain on Me (Lady Gaga feat. Ariana Grande) • Say So (Doja Cat) • and more.

00355553 . . . . $14.99

Also available:

00302274 **Top Hits of 2019** $14.99

Ukulele: The Most Requested Songs

Strum & Sing Series
Cherry Lane Music
Nearly 50 favorites all expertly arranged for ukulele! Includes: Bubbly • Build Me Up, Buttercup • Cecilia • Georgia on My Mind • Kokomo • L-O-V-E • Your Body Is a Wonderland • and more.

02501453 . . . . $14.99

The Ultimate Ukulele Fake Book

Uke enthusiasts will love this giant, spiral-bound collection of over 400 songs for uke! Includes: Crazy • Dancing Queen • Downtown • Fields of Gold • Happy • Hey Jude • 7 Years • Summertime • Thinking Out Loud • Thriller • Wagon Wheel • and more.

00175500 9" x 12" Edition $45.00
00319997 5.5" x 8.5" Edition $39.99

HAL•LEONARD®

Order today from your favorite music retailer at
halleonard.com

0621
479

Learn to play the
Ukulele
with these great Hal Leonard books!

Hal Leonard Ukulele Method

Book 1
by Lil' Rev

The *Hal Leonard Ukulele Method* is designed for anyone just learning to play ukulele. This comprehensive and easy-to-use beginner's guide by acclaimed performer and uke master Lil' Rev includes many fun songs of different styles to learn and play. The accompanying audio contains 46 tracks of songs for demonstration and play along. Includes: types of ukuleles, tuning, music reading, melody playing, chords, strumming, scales, tremolo, music notation and tablature, a variety of music styles, ukulele history and much more.

00695847 Book Only $6.99
00695832 Book/Online Audio $10.99
00320534 DVD $14.95

Book 2
00695948 Book Only $6.99
00695949 Book/Online Audio $10.99

Ukulele Chord Finder
00695803 9" x 12" $7.99
00695902 6" x 9" $6.99
00696472 Book 1 with Online Audio + Chord Finder $15.99

Ukulele Scale Finder
00696378 9" x 12" $6.99

Easy Songs for Ukulele
00695904 Book/Online Audio $14.99
00695905 Book $7.99

Ukulele for Kids
00696468 Book/Online Audio $12.99
00244855 Method & Songbook $19.99

Baritone Ukulele Method – Book 1
00696564 Book/Online Audio $10.99

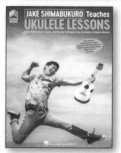

Jake Shimabukuro Teaches Ukulele Lessons
Learn notes, chords, songs, and playing techniques from the master of modern ukulele! In this unique book with online video, Jake Shimabukuro will get you started on playing the ukulele. The book includes full transcriptions of every example, the video features Jake teaching you everything you need to know plus video of Jake playing all the examples.
00320992 Book/Online Video $19.99

Fretboard Roadmaps – Ukulele
The Essential Patterns That All the Pros Know and Use
by Fred Sokolow & Jim Beloff
Take your uke playing to the next level! Tunes and exercises in standard notation and tab illustrate each technique. Absolute beginners can follow the diagrams and instruction step-by-step, while intermediate and advanced players can use the chapters non-sequentially to increase their understanding of the ukulele. The audio includes 59 demo and play-along tracks.
00695901 Book/Online Audio $14.99

Play Ukulele Today!
A Complete Guide to the Basics
by Barrett Tagliarino
This is the ultimate self-teaching method for ukulele! Includes audio with full demo tracks and over 60 great songs. You'll learn: care for the instrument; how to produce sound; reading music notation and rhythms; and more.
00699638 Book/Online Audio $10.99
00293927 Book 1 & 2/Online Media $19.99

Ukulele Aerobics
For All Levels, from Beginner to Advanced
by Chad Johnson
This package provides practice material for every day of the week and includes an online audio access code for all the workouts in the book. Techniques covered include: strumming, fingerstyle, slides, bending, damping, vibrato, tremolo and more.
00102162 Book/Online Audio $19.99

All About Ukulele
A Fun and Simple Guide to Playing Ukulele
by Chad Johnson
If you wish there was a fun and engaging way to motivate you in your uke playing quest, then this is it: All About Ukulele is for you. Whether it's learning to read music, playing in a band, finding the right instrument, or all of the above, this enjoyable guide will help you.
00233655 Book/Online Audio $19.99

HAL•LEONARD®
www.halleonard.com

Prices, contents and availability subject to change without notice. Prices listed in U.S. funds.

HAL•LEONARD® UKULELE PLAY-ALONG

AUDIO ACCESS INCLUDED

Now you can play your favorite songs on your uke with great-sounding backing tracks to help you sound like a bona fide pro! The audio also features playback tools so you can adjust the tempo without changing the pitch and loop challenging parts.

1. POP HITS
00701451 Book/CD Pack...............$15.99

2. UKE CLASSICS
00701452 Book/CD Pack...............$15.99

3. HAWAIIAN FAVORITES
00701453 Book/Online Audio $14.99

4. CHILDREN'S SONGS
00701454 Book/Online Audio $14.99

5. CHRISTMAS SONGS
00701696 Book/CD Pack...............$12.99

6. LENNON & MCCARTNEY
00701723 Book/Online Audio $12.99

7. DISNEY FAVORITES
00701724 Book/Online Audio $12.99

8. CHART HITS
00701745 Book/CD Pack...............$15.99

9. THE SOUND OF MUSIC
00701784 Book/CD Pack...............$14.99

10. MOTOWN
00701964 Book/CD Pack...............$12.99

11. CHRISTMAS STRUMMING
00702458 Book/Online Audio $12.99

12. BLUEGRASS FAVORITES
00702584 Book/CD Pack...............$12.99

13. UKULELE SONGS
00702599 Book/CD Pack...............$12.99

14. JOHNNY CASH
00702615 Book/CD Pack...............$15.99

15. COUNTRY CLASSICS
00702834 Book/CD Pack...............$12.99

16. STANDARDS
00702835 Book/CD Pack...............$12.99

17. POP STANDARDS
00702836 Book/CD Pack...............$12.99

18. IRISH SONGS
00703086 Book/Online Audio $12.99

19. BLUES STANDARDS
00703087 Book/CD Pack...............$12.99

20. FOLK POP ROCK
00703088 Book/CD Pack...............$12.99

21. HAWAIIAN CLASSICS
00703097 Book/CD Pack...............$12.99

22. ISLAND SONGS
00703098 Book/CD Pack...............$12.99

23. TAYLOR SWIFT – 2ND EDITION
00221966 Book/Online Audio $16.99

24. WINTER WONDERLAND
00101871 Book/CD Pack...............$12.99

25. GREEN DAY
00110398 Book/CD Pack...............$14.99

26. BOB MARLEY
00110399 Book/Online Audio $14.99

27. TIN PAN ALLEY
00116358 Book/CD Pack...............$12.99

28. STEVIE WONDER
00116736 Book/CD Pack...............$14.99

29. OVER THE RAINBOW & OTHER FAVORITES
00117076 Book/Online Audio $14.99

30. ACOUSTIC SONGS
00122336 Book/CD Pack...............$14.99

31. JASON MRAZ
00124166 Book/CD Pack...............$14.99

32. TOP DOWNLOADS
00127507 Book/CD Pack...............$14.99

33. CLASSICAL THEMES
00127892 Book/Online Audio $14.99

34. CHRISTMAS HITS
00128602 Book/CD Pack...............$14.99

35. SONGS FOR BEGINNERS
00129009 Book/Online Audio $14.99

36. ELVIS PRESLEY HAWAII
00138199 Book/Online Audio $14.99

37. LATIN
00141191 Book/Online Audio $14.99

38. JAZZ
00141192 Book/Online Audio $14.99

39. GYPSY JAZZ
00146559 Book/Online Audio $14.99

40. TODAY'S HITS
00160845 Book/Online Audio $14.99

Prices, contents, and availability subject to change without notice.

HAL•LEONARD®
www.halleonard.com